03 YELLOW • **BOOK 8** /igh/ar/

Supersonic SOUNDS
PHONEME PRACTICE

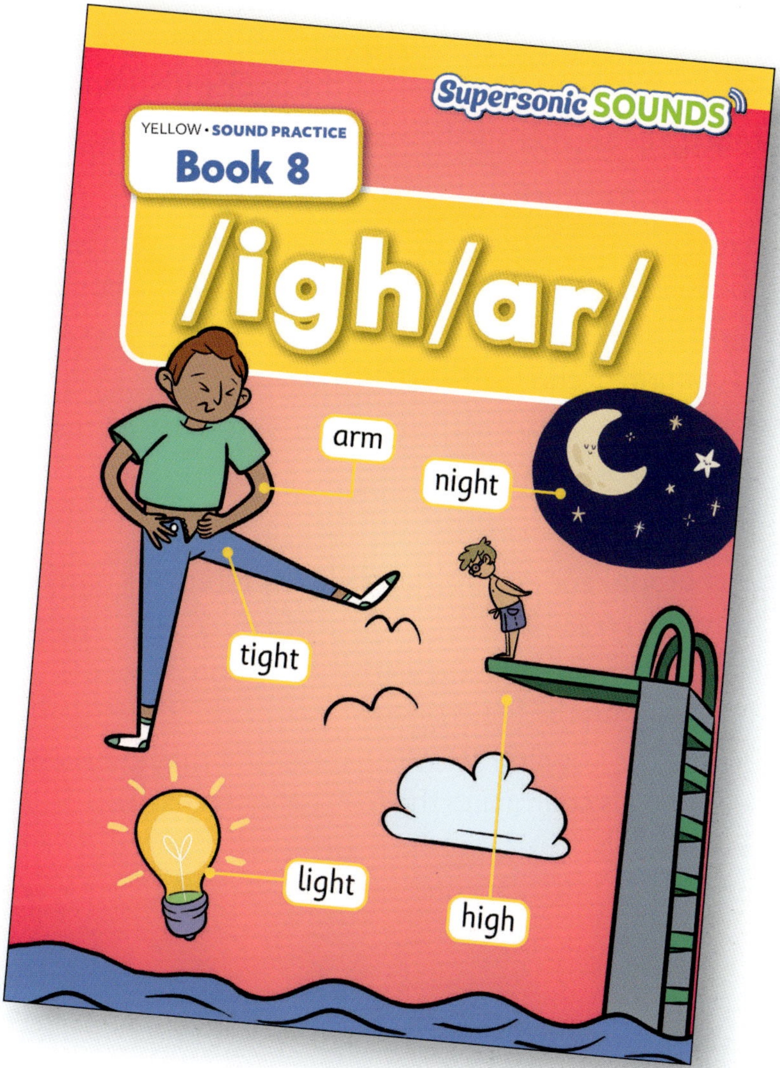

T0389857

BEARPORT PUBLISHING

Minneapolis, Minnesota

Teaching Tips

This book focuses on the phonemes **/igh/ar/**.

Getting Started

- Review the focus phonemes of the book with readers.
- Model the sounds and have readers practice themselves.

Using the Book

- Ask readers to read the words on the pages with the colorful borders, using the focus sounds as their guide.
- Turn the page and check the illustration next to the word to confirm accuracy.
- As you read new words, review the word bank on the left-hand pages of the book.

Reviewing

- Encourage readers to independently reread all of the words on pages 22–23.
- Have them complete the activity on page 24 for continued practice with the focus phonemes.
- Extend the learning by asking readers if they know any other words containing the focus phonemes.

For more information, write to Bearport Publishing, 5357 Penn Avenue South, Minneapolis, MN 55419.

night

night

night

light

light

light

night
light
high

high

high

night
light
high
tight

tight

tight

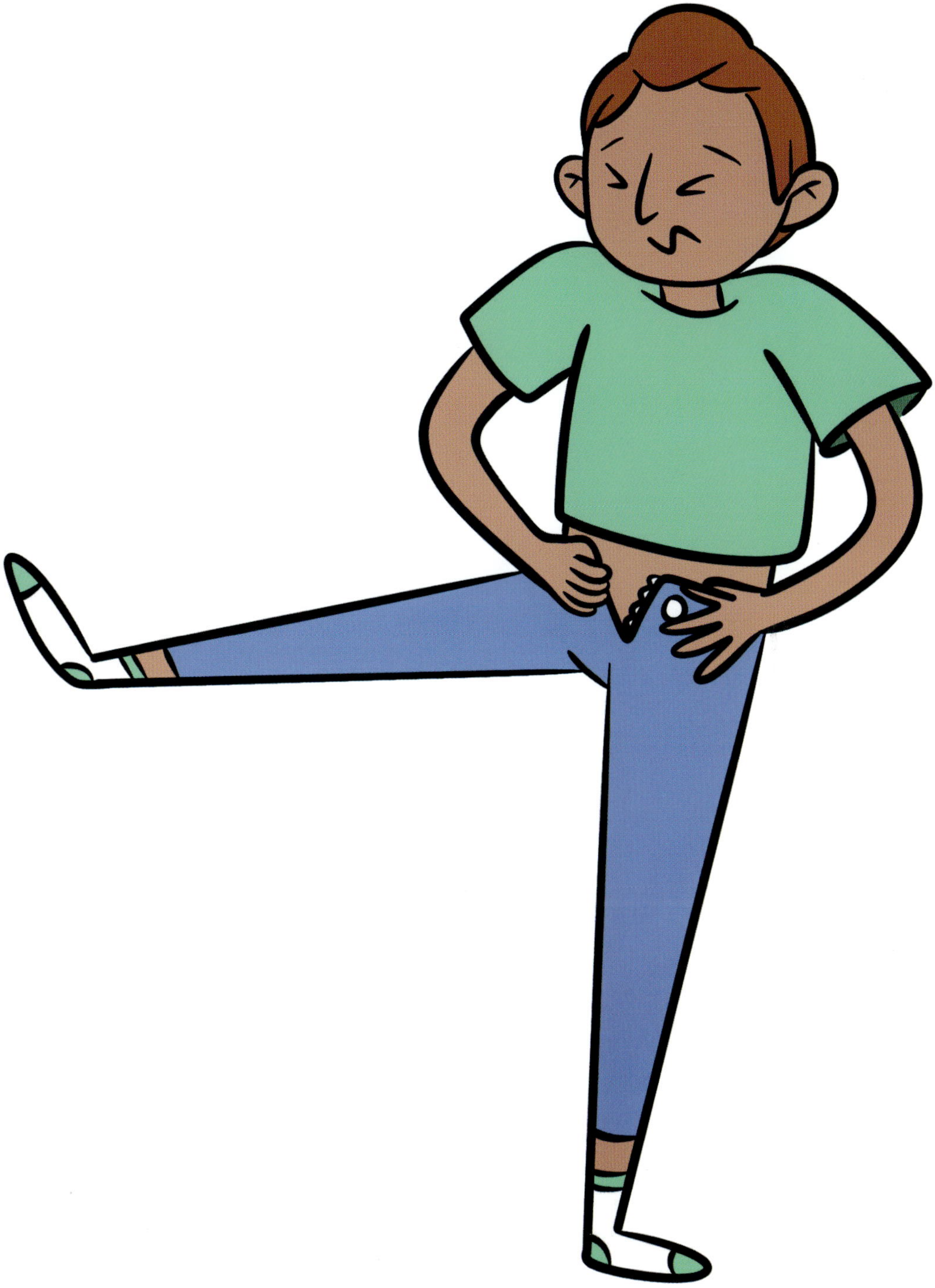

night

light

high

tight

arm

arm

arm

night

light

high

tight

arm

Say the sound and trace the letters with your finger.

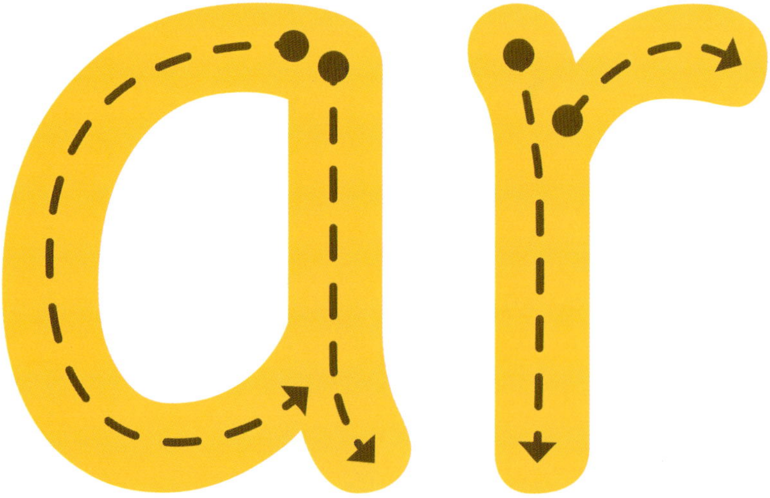